CREATE THE WEBSITE
YOU WANT WITH
WORDPRESS

ROB CUBBON LTD
LONDON SW1

Create the Website You Want with WordPress
Rob Cubbon
Published by Rob Cubbon Ltd., London. *http://robcubbon.com*
© 2014 Rob Cubbon
ISBN-13: 978-1503100282
ISBN-10: 1503100286

Contents page

Introduction

What if I told you that the biggest hurdle in creating and improving your website was in your mind?

You'd probably dismiss this immediately. "No," you might say, "I have all these technical issues to solve." But you'd be wrong. You have everything you need to start that website *right now*.

The information available on website creation is overwhelming. My mission is to stop 'analysis paralysis' in all entrepreneurs and would-be website owners.

The paralysis partly comes from choices – there's just too darn many of them! Paralysis also arises from the fear of doing something wrong. Setting up and maintaining a website, if not a huge financial investment, is a huge time investment. You'll want to make the correct choices right from the start; why get off on the wrong foot, especially if you're new to the field?

I'm here to tell you *not to worry*. Yes, you will make the wrong choices; you are human after all. But it doesn't matter. Mistakes can be rectified, and I will show you how.

Websites are the same as humans: they are living and breathing, they can change at any time and they can improve. You can transformchange the design, the content, the web host, the functionality and you can even change the domain name. In fact, I changed the domain of a website and, as a result of a global redirect, I didn't lose any of the substantial traffic and following that it had built up.

So it's time to stop analyzing and start doing. After reading this booklet, you'll be able to go out there and just get on with it. **You can do it!**

Still not convinced? Here are a few doubts you may have, which :

I'm not sure whether I should have a website: if you don't have a website, you need one. I don't care whether you're at school, you're working, you're unemployed or you're Richard Branson – you need a website. Essentially, you're irrelevant if you're not putting out content.

I don't know which hosting package to buy: This really doesn't matter. Yes, it's important, but you can change it at any time. You can either upgrade if your website increases in popularity, or you can move hosts if you think you've made the wrong decision. The new host will sometimes transfer the website free of charge.

I'm not technical, I won't be able to successfully maintain a website: You don't need to know HTML, CSS, PHP or be a technical whizz to be able to run a successful and beautiful website. I will show you how to do that in this booklet.

I'm not sure what to call the website: it depends on what you mean by 'call'. There is the domain, of course, the 'www. something.com'. Yes, this is important. But as I mentioned earlier, it can be changed. Then there's the title of the website: the name that's written on the top of the browser window, when visiting the home page. This can also be changed whenever you want.

I'm not sure what design or look and feel to go with: your website's design is almost completely separate from its content.

The design files (CSS) are different from the web pages' content files (HTML). And don't worry, I'm not going to get all technical on you. But this means that the design can be changed easily and at any time, while the content remains the same.

But what will I put on my website when there's already so much out there? I know, this may seem like a reasonable doubt, but you're forgetting the personal nature of the Internet. People like people. Certain people will prefer to get information from you. And that's powerful.

Hopefully, you're beginning to believe me when I say that the biggest hurdle is in your mind. The best thing to do is to get going. If you keep reading, I'll allay all your fears so that you can finally move forward with this.

My website is at *http://robcubbon.com* – you should check it out and let me know what you think. I keep a blog there and I would like to invite you to follow me on my journey, by **signing up for my free newsletter** at: *http://robcubbon.com/free*. (You can unsubscribe at any time.)

If you subscribe, you get free copies of my e-book PDFs: ***How to Market Yourself Online*** and ***Starting An Online Business***, two MP3s about online business, a list of my favorite online tools, plus notification of free future Kindle books and offers.

If you're interested, sign up here: *http://robcubbon.com/free.* If not, that's cool too!

Purpose

Every website should have one main purpose. And that purpose needs to be really simple. Here are some examples of aims that your website could have:

- To get potential customers to contact you about the services you offer
- To sell products
- To collect email addresses
- To raise awareness of your brand (brand building)

If your website's purpose is all of the above, then you need to rethink this. You will be more successful if you choose one main purpose.

Once you have secured a definite goal for your website, creating it and working on it will be easier. This is not to say that your website can't have multiple purposes (sell products *and* collect emails), but focusing on one will clear your thinking and make progress easier.

The creation of a website is an incredibly exciting task. You can change the world for the better with it. I don't mean you need to lock yourself in the bathroom and spend 30 minutes thinking about your purpose. To find a purpose, you need to periodically look into yourself and ask what is important to you. If it's money, fine. But usually, helping people and making a positive impact is more inspirational than short-term material gain.

And, as always, your purpose can change in the future as your website and business mature. I monitor my purposes, business goals and personal aims every three months on my blog. In the meantime, work out what it is that you are trying to achieve and stick to that. This is solid business advice.

Target market

Similar to the website's purpose is the target market. Maybe you already know your purpose and target market, so you might want to skip this, but I urge you not to.

If you think your target market is 'everyone', then I suggest you re-evaluate. Unless you expect to build the next Facebook or Twitter, then you'll need to be specific as possible with your niche choice.

It could be that your niche is you (or people like you) – this is good.

In the summer of 2005, I was a poorly-motivated freelance typesetter, plodding through tiresome company reports and hoping for each workday to end as quickly as possible. I didn't have much of a life, but I had a niche that I could work with. I started a website, RobCubbon.com, and wrote a blog about graphic design. The rest, as they say, is history. Within two years of catering to that niche, I was able to stop working on those dreadful company reports and work from home on my online business.

And, just as important as the target market, is *pain*. Allow me to explain.

Try to identify potential pain points of this target market. What are their struggles, what's keeping them up at night, what do they need or want?

My freelance graphic designers' pain points were issues with design software, the correct hardware to use, designing tips and, most importantly, "How do I get better work so I never have to typeset a company report again?" Now that's pain! It turned out that there were enough people who found that my site could heal their pain. This means there were enough people to buy products and services from me, so I could start my online business.

If you don't have a target market with a pain that you can heal, your website won't go anywhere.

Elevator pitch – who are you and who do you help?

You've got your purpose and your target market nailed down. This next section only applies if your website is about you: the 'personal' website, the online business card, the digital home. If so, your elevator pitch is very important.

The phrase 'elevator pitch' describes the following scenario: you happen to meet someone important (in an elevator, for example), and you only have seconds to introduce yourself.

"Hi, my name's Kai Winter and I'm a personal trainer" is an elevator pitch. Only it's not a very good one. Sure, it says a bit about Kai's brand and purpose. But it doesn't set the world alight.

"Hi, my name's Kai Winter and I'm passionate about showing

successful business people how to look after themselves physically and spiritually" is better; it explains Kai's purpose and it niches down into his target market and its pain point. Still, it might be a bit airy-fairy for some.

"Hi, my name's Kai Winter and I can make you more attractive to the opposite sex" hits home very hard, but isn't specific to his target market. Anyway, you get the idea.

Me? My boring elevator pitch has been: *"Hi, I'm Rob, I'm a graphic and web designer."*

I've put a lot of thought into it and I realize I'm really passionate about getting people to be successful online: *"Hi, I'm Rob, I can help you develop a personal brand and following."* It's not niche-specific, but I'm working on it.

I'm also thinking of something like: *"Hi, I'm Rob, I want to inspire you to find greater financial and personal freedom."*

Do you have an elevator pitch? Is it niche-specific? Can you incorporate it into your 'About Me' page? Is it focused on the needs of others?

Competition

I'm nearly finished with my preamble. I hope I've quelled a few doubts and worries you may have about websites. The purpose of this book is to demonstrate the ease with which websites can be created and then changed.

I've thought long and hard about this sub-heading, 'Competition', because I don't think you should be overly concerned with it. However, checking out the competition may be useful. Just don't spend too much time on it!

If there is no competition, it may be good for you, although you should seriously consider why. Is it because you've stumbled upon a great niche that no one else has thought of? Or is there nothing going on with this market? You've got to pay the bills, remember.

Still, it's likely that there is competition; try not to worry about it – it simply might mean that there is a market for more websites in your chosen area. Start by identifying the competition.

When you've done that... DON'T copy it!

First, observe the competition: notice what it does well and what it does badly. How can you improve on it? Don't be too exuberant in your criticism; it may be that some of your 'competitors' are actually friends, as the online space can be mutually supportive.

Like I said earlier, people like people. Don't worry if there's a website where somebody has already explained what you want to explain and talked about what you want to talk about. You are different from your 'competitor'. Some people will prefer to hear your explanations and discussions rather than those of your competitor. Because you're you, and some people will like *you*.

When it comes down to it, do what you love.

Platforms

When people first start thinking about their web presence, they can be very easily diverted from their course.

I constantly work with entrepreneurs who've done their homework and are full of questions about Facebook groups, affiliate commissions, Tumblr, Twitter, video and so on. My job is always to simplify their approach. It's not easy, as people are often distracted by the latest shiny object.

Whether you are just starting out online, creating a new website or if you are seeking to improve an online presence, one thing is important: focus.

My job is to **focus** the client on one or two things, and to ignore everything else that is competing for their attention. Yes, social media is important, but it can also be a terrible waste of time.

Generally, people should concentrate on two things: their website and email list. But they don't. Your website (or blog) and email list are probably the two hardest things to start working on. It's easy to get your people to follow you on Twitter or to get 'likes' on Facebook, but maintaining a blog and creating a subscriber base takes a bit of effort. So people continue to chase 'quick fix' results on social media and neglect the longer-term foundations of the site and the list.

Why are the site and the list so important? Simple, they belong to you – not anyone else.

Those of us who've been marketing online for years can agree on one word to describe our experiences – 'change'. There's not much you can be certain about in this world, but one thing you can be sure of is change.

The Internet is a graveyard of failed ventures, some of them initially successful. The changes to the Google algorithm, the introduction of Facebook's EdgeRank, the demise of Posterous and Myspace – these are all examples of sudden events that wiped away many people's incomes overnight. Don't be one of those unfortunate souls!

Your site and your list is your shield against the unpredictable forces of the Net.

Your site is yours. Your list is yours. Whereas Facebook, Twitter, YouTube and the Google algorithm don't belong to you.

With your website, you own the domain name, and the site's database and files are hosted on a professional web server that you can hire. No one can wrestle your domain away from you; even if you forget to re-register, it's kept for you for free for 90 days. Your website's files and database will be backed up daily and can be moved to any other web host at the drop of a hat.

Similarly, you can download all the email addresses in your email list at any time. Even if you're using a professional web marketing company like MailChimp or AWeber to send your email campaigns (and I recommend that you do), you still own that email list.

Therefore, your list and site are your own pieces of web real estate. They are the foundations on which your audience and authority are built. Most of your time and effort should be focused here.

How do you do this? Typically, it's with a self-hosted

WordPress blog. Don't confuse this with WordPress.com. The latter is just another blogging platform like Blogger. Whatever you want to do with your website, there's a 99% chance that WordPress will provide the best content management system (CMS) for you.

What is WordPress? WordPress is an open-source (and therefore free) blogging software which has become the most ubiquitous CMS on the Internet. Over 20% of the world's top 100,000 websites use WordPress. That's pretty impressive, especially when you consider that WordPress is almost wholly maintained by volunteers.

Given the highly motivated community behind it, WordPress provides an excellent and easy to use back-end to simplify the complex computer code behind a website. Using WordPress means that you don't have to learn code – it does the heavy lifting for you. And if you have a problem, someone else will have had the same problem and there will be a solution already written out to help you.

Solutions to WordPress problems sometimes come in the form of plug-ins. Plug-ins are extensions you can add onto WordPress to provide extra functionality. There's a plug-in for everything: from contact forms and 'buy' buttons, to email capture forms, you can just use someone else's ready-made solution.

Now you have the software you need to run your website and you haven't even spent a penny. It's WordPress, and you can download it now at *WordPress.org*. Next, you'll need a domain name and a web host. We'll come to that.

Summary

Lots of things can be changed later – design, content, host, domain name, etc. – so it's important not to let 'analysis paralysis' delay action on creating your website. Just do it!

- Your website should have a specific simple purpose
- Your website should have a target market
- If your website is for your own personal brand, you should start thinking about your 'elevator pitch'
- Monitor websites within the same niche as yours, but don't copy them
- Use WordPress as the content management system (not WordPress.com)

Domain name

The domain name is the 'something.com' in the 'www.something.com' of your website's address.

This is the only decision you should spend time thinking about. As I've said before, many things about your website can be changed, including the domain name, but changing the domain name after your website has gone live is a hassle and damaging to your brand, so it would be better to get it right the first time.

Choosing the extension (.com, .net, etc.)

I would always prefer a dot com (.com). Google gives a slight preference to domains with a .com extension. It looks professional and international.

If you really can't find anything you like as a .com, then my second choice would be a dot net (.net). People have made a success of .net; ProBlogger.net springs to mind.

I advise against using country-specific domains like '.co.uk' for the UK or '.co.nz' for New Zealand, etc., unless you're absolutely sure that your business will always be relevant to only one country.

Types of domain names

When choosing a domain name for a branded website, you have several choices:

- use your name
- use your company's name

- use 'keywords'
- use neutral words
- use a combination of the above

To start at the top, my main website is RobCubbon.com – it's my first and last name. It has served me well, because it means that I can blog about lots of different things. It's important to stick to a niche or the particular subject you specialize in. However, if you use your name, you are free to move into slightly different areas of interest.

Or you could use your company's name for the domain. This would have the same advantages as using your name. A company isn't as constant in your life as your name is, though. You better make sure you don't ever go bust and the company in question is yours.

Alternatively, you could go for 'keywords'. Keywords are what people type into search engines to find content on the Internet. An example of a domain with keywords in the title is SmartPassiveIncome.com, a blog belonging to an amazing blogger and entrepreneur called Pat Flynn.

Adding keywords to the domain of a website has certain advantages. For a start, it's immediately obvious what the site is about. You can guess what the website SmartPassiveIncome.com is about from the domain name. The disadvantage would be that the site owner couldn't diverge from the area or niche of the site's content. However there's another, more important benefit in having keywords in the domain. They give your site an advantage in search engines' results pages. If you have the keywords 'passive income' in the domain, you are more likely to show up in search results for those keywords.

If your name, your company name or your keywords aren't available, you may want to go for 'neutral' words. An example of this would be ViperChill.com, belonging to one of my favorite bloggers – Glen Allsopp – who writes about SEO and online marketing. The words themselves don't have any meaning at all. But in the absence of good keywords or a name, it's a good alternative. Neutral words create a brand as much as your name or keywords. A domain of neutral words can be sold to someone else. This would be almost impossible if you use your own name.

Lastly, you could use a combination of your own name, your company name, keywords or neutral words.

Choosing your domain name

In the past, I've been guilty of thinking that all the good .com domains have been taken. But this is just not true. There are several fantastic sites where you can enter a keyword and choose from the hundreds of available .com domains that their engine comes up with. One of them is *leandomainsearch.com*

A domain name should be short, contain only letters (without hyphens, numbers or non-alphabetical symbols) and ideally have a .com extension. Most importantly, pick a memorable domain name. Pick a domain that, when you say it, most people can easily type correctly into a browser's address bar.

However, as with everything else when you are creating a new website, don't worry about it too much. It may require extra effort, but it can be changed. Don't let indecision over a domain name stop you from taking action.

It's more important to get your website live, published, indexed by search engines and visible to millions of humans around the world. And I'm going to tell you how to do just that.

Register the domain name

In order to go live with a website, you need two things – and neither should cost you much money. First you need to register your domain name and second, you need web hosting.

Registering a domain typically costs about $10/year. It doesn't matter who you choose to register your domain name with. I used to use GoDaddy, which is usually pretty cheap although some of its marketing leaves a bad taste in the mouth. You could also use Namecheap or any other company to do this.

The only choice you need to consider carefully is how many years to register it for. If you are purchasing a domain name for your own branded website, then I would advise that you register it for at least five years.

This might save you a bit of money in the long run but, more importantly, Google likes domains that are registered for years into the future because it sends a message that this website will be around for a while and isn't a fly-by-night venture.

So just go for it – register that domain! We're talking $10 a year. It's not going to break the bank.

Hosting

Now that we've decided on a domain name, there's only one more thing to do before the excitement starts and we can create a website. And that's finding a web host.

Commercial web hosting is a highly competitive industry and there are loads of big players that offer decent web hosting at reasonable prices. Before we discuss which host you should choose, let me first explain what different types of web hosting there are.

Shared hosting

The most basic form of hosting is shared hosting, which can be purchased for as little as $2 a month. The expression "you get what you pay for" may be accurate to explain web hosting prices, but not all of the time.

A $2/month shared hosting account may be sufficient for some website owners. A shared hosting plan means the website resides on a data server alongside hundreds or thousands of other websites. There is nothing intrinsically wrong with this, but if one of the other websites on your server gets a spike in traffic, it can slow your site down. Shared hosting can be a lottery for this reason. And there are other factors to consider.

Cheap hosts may also restrict the bandwidth and space you are allowed. The space is the combined size of your website's files, and bandwidth is the amount of information that the server will deliver. If you have lots of traffic, your monthly bandwidth could get used up and then your host will stop serving your website to visitors.

Sometimes being on a shared host can make you "guilty by association", as you could be on the same server as a porn site or something known to Google as a "bad neighborhood". However, this is unlikely to happen with some of the hosts I will be recommending.

You may want to shop around for a good deal with a reputable host such as Bluehost, HostGator or Justhost. They have been victims of their own success and have suffered hacking attacks recently, although they appear to be over them at the time of writing. I also recommend a host in the UK called Vidahost.

Please go to the resources page of this book at *http:// robcubbon.com/kindle5* to find links to recommended hosts.

Dedicated hosting

The cheapest shared hosting may be $2/month and, as discussed, you will share the server with hundreds of other sites.

With dedicated hosting, as you may have guessed, your website is sharing a web server with no one. Dedicated hosting is much more expensive and starts at around $100/month.

You are very much on your own with dedicated hosting. You pretty much own the web server for a period of time and are expected to set up the hosting software on it, monitor it, perform back-ups and security checks.

This may require more technical know-how than a lot of webmasters have, but there are other options. Dedicated hosts offer varying levels of support.

VPS hosting

A VPS (Virtual Private Server) is a halfway house between shared and dedicated hosting. On a VPS, you are allotted resources that are not shared by everyone on the same server. The overall processing power is shared across all accounts on the machine but, at the same time, portions of resources are always dedicated to each account.

As I've mentioned before, it's not the end of the world if you purchase the wrong hosting package, because you can always jump between hosts at a later date.

Setting up hosting

Now that you've got a domain name and hosting for your new baby, you need to put the two together. In order to do this, you need to change the NameServers at the domain name registrar.

This will possibly be the trickiest technical thing you'll do in your early online career, and it may take you all of two minutes.

As you can see from the above screenshot, it's a matter of finding a link entitled something like "Change NameServers" or "Configure DNS" at your domain name registrar.

Here you should enter the NameServers that have been given to you by your host. If you're not sure, you can just ask them but these should be in an introductory email you received when you signed up with the host. They'll look something like this:

ns1.hostname.com

ns2.hostname.com

In the image below, you can see the NameServers for my site at GoDaddy. In my case there are three, but usually there are only two.

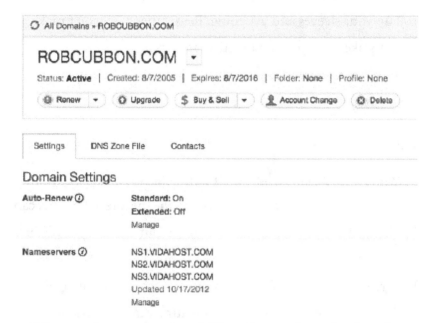

When you've put your host's NameServers in at the domain name registrar, you need to wait maybe a day (usually much less) for the change to percolate through the system.

Once you have connected your domain name to your web hosting, you are ready to start building your website. Now the fun really begins.

Setting up WordPress

You have a domain name, your branded identity online. You have a host, a place to physically put your website. And you've connected the two together. Now all you've got to do is set up WordPress, and you're good to go.

Most hosts will offer a one-click WordPress install.

If this is your first time setting up WordPress, you may find the platform a bit daunting in the beginning, but the secret is to roll up your sleeves and get going. Remember, you won't make any mistakes that you can't rectify later on.

Here are a few things you need to do or think about when you start out:

Name your blog

When you go through the WordPress installation process, you will be confronted with a screen asking for the Site Title. This can be changed later. However, you'll want to put a few keywords in here and narrow the site down to its niche. My site title used to be "Freelance Graphic Designer London", which worked really well to define my subject matter and attract targeted traffic.

This can be changed later by going to the WordPress administration area (see below), Settings > General and there you can change your Site Title. And you may as well add a Tagline while you're there.

Your Site Title and Tagline should be the keyword-rich representations of you and your business that we discussed in earlier chapters.

Create pretty permalinks

This sounds a bit nerdy, but it's something you've just got to do. In the WordPress back-end (this is something I'll be talking about constantly; it refers to when you're logged into the

WordPress administration area, and has /wp-admin/ after your domain in the browser address bar), on the left-hand side at the bottom, you'll see Settings. Under Settings, click Permalinks. And choose Post name.

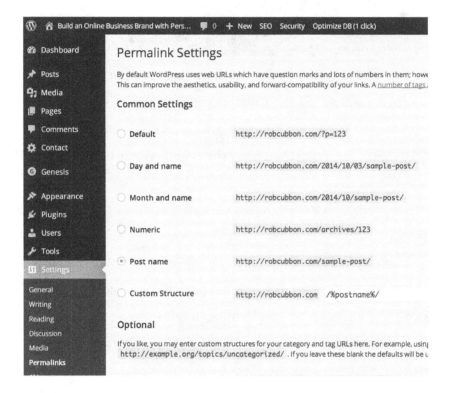

This means that all the links to your blog posts and pages are 'pretty' (for example: *domain.com/pretty-permalink*), rather than 'ugly' (for example: *domain.com/p?=38574*).

Change the admin

This strengthens your site's security. In the WordPress back-end, down the left-hand side, click Users and then Add New. Choose a new, hard to remember, Username and Password, and don't forget to select Administrator for the Role at the bottom.

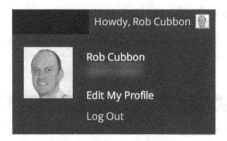

You should then log out (top right), log in as the new username you've just created and delete your old username.

You may think, "Oh Rob, why are you getting me to do all this?" Well, the number one way that WordPress is hacked is via brute force attacks through the admin login. This step gives you better protection from this particular vulnerability than 90% of WordPress sites out there.

There's plenty more to do to your WordPress install than just the above three points. But let's not push it. We've got a brand new site – and a brand new brand – to work on.

It's important that we know why we're doing this. And what we're going to do with the site. That brings us to… Content.

Content

Now, I know what you're thinking: "Rob, we've only just set up WordPress and now you're talking about content? What about design? Social media? The whole shebang?"

But my point is this: your website will live or die on content. So you may as well get started.

It doesn't matter what your website looks like because Google, especially, judges it by the words written on it. Nowadays, in particular, a successful entrepreneur needs to be able to write. And there's only one way to learn how to write. And that's by writing.

You've heard that "content is king" and you've heard about content marketing. Well, it's true and it works. But you've got to put some effort in. It's not about creating one great bit of content and sitting back. It's about creating content consistently.

There's only one way to create content consistently, and that's to love doing it. If your heart's not in it, you won't do it successfully. Create content around what you are passionate about and, here's the most important thing, try to make this a habit. So you have to develop your "content creation muscle".

For you, it might be every day. For me, it's every week. I write a blog post (article for my website) every week.

You need two things to make your new website successful: your passion/area of expertise, plus habitual content creation. Otherwise, you will lose interest.

You have a business, a business idea, a personality – most of us are passionate about one or all of these things – so it shouldn't be too difficult to create great content around this subject matter.

All of a sudden, your mind is racing: "What can I talk about, Rob? I know my business but I can't write thousands and thousands of words about it." That's what I thought when I started. But I didn't worry about it. I'm only worried about the next bit of content.

That's the beauty of blogging – it's all about your most recent post.

Can you do it? You'll never know unless you try. And you've got to keep trying.

How to create content

If you go into the WordPress back-end (also called the Dashboard), you're confronted with links down the left-hand side: Posts, Media, Pages, Comments, etc. It's good to get familiar with these.

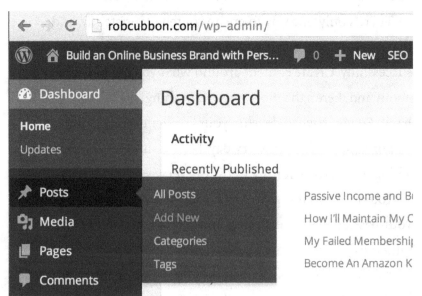

Comments are the comments on your blog – no surprises there. Media is for images, PDFs, files and those sorts of things. Don't worry about these for now.

However, you need to understand the distinction between WordPress Posts and Pages. It's very simple. WordPress Pages are for the important, static pages of your site. These are the About Me/Us page, the Contact Me/Us page, maybe a Testimonials page, etc. So the WordPress Pages here are the pages that tend to sit on your top navigational menu in the header area of your site.

The WordPress Posts, on the other hand, are for the Blog. They are the updates to the blog that you'll write frequently (hopefully). Blog Posts are the articles you put out into the world that add value.

So, in the Dashboard, go Posts > Add New and you're confronted with a page like this:

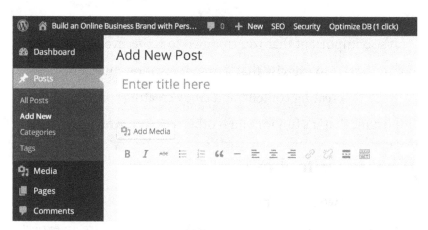

As you may have guessed, you enter a title (a relevant, keyword-rich title that people are going to be interested in) and, in the box below, you begin writing.

Then you write. And you write. You keep writing for as long as you can.

This is the secret of great writing. The first stage is 'word vomit' – don't worry about whether it's any good.

Of course, when you get further down the line, you'll want to sketch out or mind-map your blog post ideas on paper first, and have some sort of plan of attack. But, if you're just starting out, I would just write.

You may write about your initial ideas for creating a website. How do you think you will help people with it? What subjects are you going to cover? What is the purpose of the site?

Sure, the answers to these questions may change over time. That's the beauty of blogging – every post is date-stamped. If you want them to, people can see when you wrote each post. Every subject you write about can be revisited if you have more to say at a later time.

It's so important that you sit down to write, even at this early point, to start to exercise that "content creation muscle".

Keep on creating content, and *enjoy* creating content. It's very important that it's fun for you – otherwise you won't stick to it.

What to write about

Write about what you know.

Whatever your business is about. Whatever you are an expert in. Whatever area of life or work that you can help people with. Write about that.

Get specific. Drill these subjects down into sub-subjects.

No one's interested in your opinion on "small business and entrepreneurship". It's too general. But a small group of people may be fascinated by "how to make money creating video courses on Udemy", for example.

Don't worry about being so specific that few people will be interested. That's the whole point of blogging. You are aiming to be very interesting to a small group of people. Don't try to be a little bit interesting to a large group of people. You'll end up being boring.

Some of my most successful blog posts have been technical *and* specific. Here are some of the blog posts I've written that have been popular:

- Free Calendars as PDF, Illustrator and InDesign files for Download!
- Create a Free 3D E-Book Cover
- Creating & Styling Sidebar Widgets in WordPress
- How to Start a Web Design Business From Home
- How I Make $2500+ A Month From Udemy And Skillfeed
- 15 Essential Tasks to Complete after Installing WordPress

As you can see, they are quite technical. I'm not saying you have to be very technical in a blog. But I am saying *be specific.*

Be yourself. Writing a blog can be daunting at first. You read great blog posts every day from some of the best writers of our times and you think: "I can't do that! There are so many blogs out there in my niche, what content can I add that hasn't been done already?" I understand. We've all been there.

But your opinions do matter. You're you. And for that reason, what you think and what you say on a subject is unique. And the Internet loves uniqueness.

Don't ape what the 'experts' say. If someone disagrees with you, don't be afraid; it's the best thing in the world for a blogger, as that means that someone is consuming your content and having a reaction to it.

Talking about your own specific experience in business makes unique and relevant content.

Content needs to be unique and relevant.

Social media, blog promotion and relationships

This is probably a good moment to explain that just creating content isn't enough. A long time ago, in the Wild West days of the Internet (less than 10 years ago), you could get away with writing content and nothing else.

These days, you not only have to promote that content but also, hopefully, have other people promoting it for you.

So even at this early stage, you should think about engaging with an audience, not just creating content on your site. But I don't want to suggest you spend hours and hours of your time on Twitter, LinkedIn, Facebook, etc.

Social media can be a huge time-killer. If you enjoy spending hours on these social networks, then don't let me stop you. However, I wouldn't recommend social media as a sustainable traffic source or a great place to promote your content.

Try to think of as many places as possible were you can link to your website and blog posts, *but don't put links where they're not wanted!* Maybe you're active in forums and, if so, see if you can add a link in your forum signature.

Also, perhaps you can write for well-established blogs in your niche (guest blogging). At the very least, you'll be able to add your link in the author box, and maybe another one in the body of the article if it's relevant.

But the best way to promote your content is through relationships (this is so important that we'll be coming back to this later in the booklet).

Identify people who are on the same business journey as you are, but are slightly ahead or a little behind. Who really resonates with you online? Who do you admire? Who has a similar business outlook to you?

You should be connecting with these people. Leave comments on their blog, email them and, yes, connect with them on social media.

Engage with them in an interesting and *real* way; don't just say, "Hey dude, love your stuff!" Say something authentic and add value to the discussion. Then pretty soon, the emails, Skype conversations and mutual respect will flow between you two, and your new friend will share and promote your content. They may even link to you – and quality, relevant links are what Google loves.

A better way to forge these win-win business relationships is offline. Try to go to as many meetups, co-working spaces and conferences that are relevant to your business as you can. This depends on where you are in the world, but I find that Meetup. com is very useful for this.

We're all social animals. Enjoy your business relationships, talk about subjects you're passionate about, offer quality advice to your contacts and do everything you can for other people. You'll be repaid many times over.

Design

I f you're creating a branded website, then design is going to be important. But you'll notice that I haven't mentioned design much yet, even though I spent years and years in London being employed as a graphic designer.

"When are you going to start talking about design, Rob?" Yes, I hear you.

Design consistency is important for your brand's recognition. But I just don't want you to stress or spend a lot of money on it. (I know, this sounds strange coming from a designer.)

Sure, spend money – if you have it – on a good design, but I really want to stress the greater importance of content over design.

You've got your website set up and you're creating content – don't stop! Don't let design get in the way. Why? It can be changed anytime. You don't have to do it all at once. That's the beauty of websites: everything can be changed.

WordPress Themes

The way you change your WordPress website's design is via Appearance > Themes in the back-end.

A WordPress theme is like a cloak of color and formatting that will change the appearance of your site, but not the content.

In the beginning, you will only have the default themes that come with WordPress. These themes are called: Twenty Ten, Twenty Eleven, Twenty Twelve, Twenty Thirteen and Twenty Fourteen.

On the Appearance > Themes page, in the WordPress administration area of your site, you can 'Live Preview' any of the other themes or 'Activate' other themes to make your website look different. You can do this as many times as you like to get a feel for changing themes.

Choosing a theme

The default WordPress themes are secure and robust, as they have been tested thoroughly by the WordPress community before release. The only problem is that if you use one of these themes, your site will look like a lot of other sites, because many people use the default free themes that come with WordPress.

Theme selection can be a time-consuming practice. I wouldn't advise you to go to the WordPress theme repository and search through the thousands and thousands of free themes there. For one thing, you can't be sure of the quality of the themes and, secondly, there are so many to choose from that you'll go crazy.

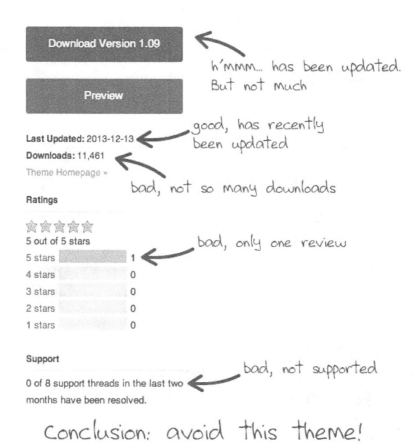

Conclusion: avoid this theme!

But if you want to try a free theme, make sure it has been downloaded many times, has been updated recently and has been supported by the theme creator in support threads. Themes that are unpopular, badly-supported and not updated are more likely to cause you problems.

A great alternative is to have a look at the sites you admire visually, and try to see which theme they are using. This may not always be possible, as most of the best WordPress sites will use a custom theme. But it's worth scrolling down to the bottom of the page and seeing if the theme is credited in the footer.

Of course, you could always contact the site owner, congratulate them on the look of their website and ask what theme they're using. (This is a great way to start one of those win-win business relationships I was talking about earlier.)

Premium themes

Most of the best websites out there would have spent a bit of money on their WordPress design. Free is great, don't get me wrong. WordPress is free. There are many great free plug-ins (which we'll come to later) and many great free themes (like the default themes). However, I would suggest you spend a bit of money on a premium theme.

Premium themes not only look better and more professional, they are also superior in terms of functionality, ease of use, security and SEO (good for Google rankings).

There are many successful premium theme companies that have emerged off the back of WordPress's success. Thesis, WooThemes and PageLines are theme shops that spring to mind.

But I would like to concentrate on one WordPress theme framework that has over 40 themes under its umbrella. That WordPress theme framework is called Genesis, created by a company called StudioPress.

It's a 'theme framework' as opposed to a theme. A theme framework sits in your WordPress theme's folder, but you actually activate the individual 'child themes' to change the theme. The child theme only contains a limited number of design, formatting and functionality settings but refers to the main 'theme framework' for most of the heavy lifting. The advantage of this framework and child theme set-up is that the framework can be updated alongside WordPress's updates, without breaking any of the changes or customizations you've made to your child theme.

Suffice it to say that after nearly 10 years of using WordPress, I'm really glad I chose this theme framework and I wouldn't work with anything else.

Here are some more reasons I use the Genesis theme framework:

- Copyblogger, 2CreateAWebsite, MattCutts, WPbeginner, ProBlogger, Chris Brogan, etc., use it (and many more big and famous WordPress sites)
- WordPress bigwigs like Mark Jaquith (security), Joost de Valk (SEO) and Matt Mullenweg (founder developer of WordPress) vouch for it
- It creates really well-marked up HTML5, which is really easy to work with
- There are super easy-to-use free plug-ins that come with it to do almost everything (image slider, meta tag and footer editing, social media profile links, email capture forms); you don't have to use them but they're there if you want them
- Mobile responsive and retina-screen ready
- Part of the Copyblogger/StudioPress stable. so you know it's going to be well-maintained and is as future-proof as anything

Those are the pros. The con is the learning curve to create custom areas in pages. You have to put PHP in the functions.php for this, but it's all superbly documented that I've never had a problem.

There's a good reason for this. If you do everything through functions.php with hooks and filters, it makes it easier for the main framework to be updated and to tag along with the core updates. It's part of the reason it's future-proof. If you don't want to do heavy customization yourself, then this won't be a problem. You can get a developer from oDesk or Elance to do this cheaply.

I recommend only the Genesis framework which is $60, and this gets you support and access to the forums.

I also recommend that you use the sample child theme, which comes free with the framework, but you can also buy individual child themes for $20-30 if you want. This is what I do. So I've never bought all the 40-odd child themes for $400 – there's no point!

But, if you don't want to buy the Genesis theme framework, here's what you should look out for in a WordPress theme.

The theme should be responsive

The theme's design must respond to the device it is being viewed on.

You can find out if a theme is responsive or not by dragging the bottom right-hand corner and resizing the browser window so that you can only see a very narrow view of the website. If the website responds to the different widths, then the theme is responsive to smartphones and tablets.

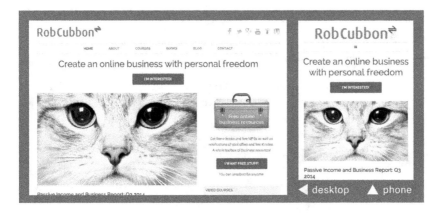

As you know, more and more content is being viewed on phones these days, so this is very important.

Threaded comments and featured images

Here are another two WordPress theme features that I would insist on when choosing a new theme – threaded comments and featured images.

The option to allow people to leave comments is on by default when you set up WordPress – and I'd advise you to keep it that way. To the outside world, having lots of comments after a blog post makes it look as if a website is inspiring engagement and discussion.

Threaded or nested comments are when people, as well as the author, can respond to a certain comment by hitting reply.

Threaded comments are more likely to increase engagement, so I would always choose a theme with them.

Erwin says
July 1, 2014 at 2:56 am (Edit)

wow! Thanks Rob, this is very timely as I started to collect emails, just launch 2 months ago my English-Filipino blog site. And your mentioning of your membership site excite me as I'm planning to launch my own membership site next month (my 1st online product offer) … excited and nervous, haha. Anyway, thanks again for this very helpful tips Rob.

Reply

Rob Cubbon says
July 1, 2014 at 10:38 am (Edit)

Hey Erwin, thanks for the comment. Best of luck with your membership site. It's definitely a challenge but well worth it as well. Glad you found the tips helpful.

Reply

Erwin says
July 1, 2014 at 10:48 am (Edit)

Do you have any excellent resource post about "How To Create or Manage Membership site? Or any recommended post about it? Thank you Rob.

Reply

Featured/thumbnail images

If you arrive on a web page, and you see lines and lines of text, what do you do? Even if the content is the best in the world, it's likely that you'll get bored and leave the site, never to return. So, *always add images to every page on your site.*

All well and good.

But with WordPress sites, you also have archive pages. Archive pages are the pages that list your blog posts. There are many type of archive pages: they can be pages that list the blog posts in a certain category; pages that list your blog posts by a certain author; they can be the search results; and even the home page, by default, lists your most recent blog posts.

The best treatment of these pages is like this: show the titles of the blog posts with excerpts and featured images.

Passive Income and Business Report: Q3 2014

 We are now at the end of the third quarter of the year. It's time to add up all the passive income I've received in the last three months and to look ahead to see where my business is going. I publish my results (along with cat photos) every quarter and, I'm pretty sure, ... [Read more...]

How I'll Maintain My Online Business While Abroad

 I'm leaving for Thailand soon and I'm stupidly excited. However, my childish enthusiasm is tempered by the niggling doubt of how the hell I'm going to make money while I'm there! So here are some of the tools and practices I'm going to employ to ensure the smooth ... [Read more...]

My Failed Membership Site Launch – Lessons Learned

 Running an online business is fun. But some days you feel like you're drowning. Just when you think you know something, that's when life will slap you in the face and show that you, in fact, know nothing. What is my membership site? I spent months and over $600 ... [Read more...]

Showing featured images makes the archive pages look better. I would only choose a theme that has the ability to show featured images and excerpts on archive pages.

Customizing your theme

The best option you have to create a professional-looking, branded website is to customize a premium theme. You'll get the best of both worlds – all the flexibility, security and support that a premium theme provides plus, with a few inexpensive design tweaks, you'll get a website with its own individual look and feel.

You can do a lot of the customization by yourself, via the back-end of the theme. The Genesis child themes have their own plug-ins, where you can successfully edit areas of the site like the sidebar and the footer.

Also, the Genesis themes have a lot of 'widgetized' areas. WordPress widgets are self-contained bits of website code that can be applied to a widgetized area via an easy-to-use, drag-and-drop interface; this can be found in the back-end at Appearance > Widgets.

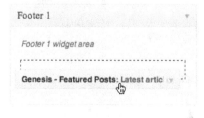

Within seconds, you can add search bars, email sign-up forms, featured posts, etc., into certain areas, without having to ask a professional.

How far you go down the customization route depends on your budget. Look at my site – RobCubbon.com – it is a customized version of Magazine Pro, a Genesis/StudioPress child theme. I changed a few fonts, text sizes and colors here and there (Genesis themes can come with three or four color schemes that you can change yourself).

It shouldn't be too expensive to get this sort of customization done to a Genesis child theme like Magazine Pro (minus a new logo). I would head over to oDesk or Elance and find a developer with Genesis experience, good ratings and general experience with the site, for $9-19/hour.

Getting a logo designed

As a graphic designer, I'm about to say something sacrilegious and something that'll get you lynched on a design forum. For your logo, I'd probably use *99Designs.com.*

I've never used it myself, but I hear great things about this crowdsourcing design site. However, there is certainly a right way and a wrong way to commission a logo. And, remember, you could also find a designer on Elance or oDesk.

The instructions you give to the designer (or potential designer) are:

- The logo should be provided in high resolution format, preferably as an Adobe Illustrator AI; if not, as a PSD on a transparent background
- Make sure the logo can satisfactorily appear on a white background

- The logo should not include any photographic imagery and should be made up of shapes, colors or gradients only
- If your chosen premium theme has an optimum size for the logo, make sure you communicate that specific size to the logo designer. Using my Genesis Magazine Pro child theme as an example, images of exactly 380x90 pixels will give the best results.

Make sure you communicate the above specifics to the logo designer.

Additionally, you'll need to communicate the 'look and feel' you want to the designer. You can do this by preparing a logo brief document. The logo brief document should include:

- The purpose of the website
- The target audience of the website
- Examples of other websites you like and think are right for your brand
- A mood board on Pinterest. (A mood board consists of all sorts of images that communicate the brand. They can be textures, photography, typography, colors, anything. The images won't be used in the project, but they give the designer an idea of the 'mood' or 'culture' of the company or individual they are working for.)
- Examples of other logos you like and think are right for your brand

The logo decision is one of the most important design decisions you'll ever make. Don't be afraid of spending some money on it. I would consider $250 to be the bare minimum to spend on a logo, and I'd be happy to spend much more.

Remember, keep it simple and make sure it's on a white background.

Colors

Your logo should consist of one main color and, ideally, a secondary color. These colors are extremely important as they will be the colors that represent your brand.

At the end of the design process, you should ask your designer for the hexadecimal reference for the primary and secondary colors in your logo. This is a numerical code (sometimes with an alphabetical letter) preceded by the # sign.

You will use these colors elsewhere on your site and in your design collateral (books, leaflets, business cards, etc.). This is why you need the color reference from the designer – so that you can accurately recreate it.

Later on, you will use these colors on your social media platforms, so that your whole output has the same consistent branding.

WordPress essentials

We touched on WordPress earlier. We learned the difference between Pages (static pages, like the Contact page) and Posts (blog posts). We've also touched on featured images. But there is more to learn about WordPress to run a successful blog and authoritative web presence. I can hear you complaining, "oh Rob, why do we have to do this boring stuff?" I'm sorry. This stuff is important.

This isn't an exhaustive list, but I am going to go into some detail. So bear with me, because it's important that your WordPress site looks good, behaves well and attracts people – especially customers.

A lot of these WordPress essentials come in the form of plug-ins. WordPress plug-ins are bits of software that can be easily added to WordPress to expand the functionality of your site.

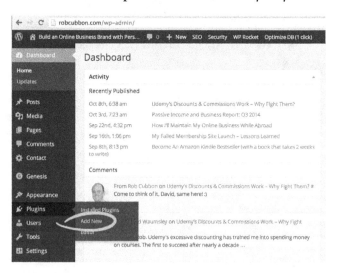

It's easy to install a plug-in. Go to Plugins > Add New in the WordPress back-end. You then search for the name of the plug-in you want to install and, remember, don't forget to Activate it after you Install it.

Most plug-ins then require you to change their settings to ensure the desired performance.

XML Sitemap

One of the most important challenges for websites is getting found on Google. An XML Sitemap is a tiny file that sits on the web server next to your site and, as its name suggests, is a 'map' of the site's pages.

It's particularly useful because if it's registered with Google, it will inform the search engine when new pages are added, making sure your site is indexed properly and quickly.

In order to create an XML Sitemap for the first time and ensure that it automatically updates in the future, you need to install a plug-in. I use Google Sitemap Generation plug-in: *https://wordpress.org/plugins/google-sitemap-generator*.

Google Webmaster Tools

Once your sitemap is generated, you should register it with Google Webmaster Tools. It's possible that Google and the other search engines will find your sitemap, but as Google Webmaster Tools provides you with other great tools, it's great to register your site there anyway: *https://www.google.com/webmasters/tools*.

Check back with Google Webmaster Tools a day or so after you've registered your sitemap, and you'll see that Google has indexed all of your pages.

Google Webmaster Tools also gives you valuable information about the keywords you are ranking for. Plus, it will alert you if it suspects your site has a virus and if your site contains any broken links or errors.

Google Analytics

Google Analytics is another hugely useful free service from Google. It gives you the indispensable information of how many people visited your site at a specific time, what pages they viewed, for how long and so much more. Most people use Google Analytics for visitor statistics.

You can go to Google Analytics (*http://www.google.com/ analytics*) and set up an account, and you'll be given a tracking code that you need to put on every page of your website. This is very easy with WordPress. If you are using the Genesis theme, go to Genesis > Theme Settings in the WordPress back-end, and you can enter anything under the Header and Footer Scripts. Paste your tracking code in the first box, and then the code will sit at the beginning of the HTML of every page in your website.

Header and Footer Scripts

Enter scripts or code you would like output to `wp_head()` :

```
<script>
(function(i,s,o,g,r,a,m){i['GoogleAnalyticsObject']=r;i[r]=i[r]||function(){
(i[r].q=i[r].q||[]).push(arguments)},i[r].l=1*new Date();a=s.createElement(o),
m=s.getElementsByTagName(o)[0];a.async=1;a.src=g;m.parentNode.insertBefore(a,m)
})(window,document,'script','//www.google-analytics.com/analytics.js','ga');

ga('create', 'UA-803779-1', 'robcubbon.com');
ga('send', 'pageview');
```

The `wp_head()` hook executes immediately before the closing `</head>` tag in the document source.

After a few hours, you will start to see your visitor statistics. I check my Google Analytics almost every day. For me this is essential market research information, provided by the most powerful search engine company, on a minute-by-minute basis.

SEO (titles)

We have touched on keywords and SEO already. SEO stands for Search Engine Optimization, and is the practice of making your website 'search engine friendly', so that you are returned in as many online searches as possible.

SEO is broken down into two parts: on site and off site. Off-site SEO is largely to do with links to your website. On-site optimization involves organizing the material on your website in a way that the search engines prefer.

The most important on-page SEO factor is the page title. Page titles are seen at the top of the browser window (if not on Chrome, you have to click 'Window' on the menu bar, and you will see the title at the bottom of the drop-down).

You should optimize your page titles so that they are accurate descriptions of that page's content, and so that they contain keywords.

If you're using Genesis, you have complete control over the SEO settings and titles in the back-end.

Alternatively there's a plug-in that will help you with this: Yoast's WordPress SEO: *https://wordpress.org/plugins/wordpress-seo*. This plug-in gives you complete control. You can create unique page titles and meta descriptions for all your archives and category pages, as well as for all other posts and pages. It also helps you with setting up Google Webmaster Tools, Facebook Open Graph meta data, Twitter card meta data and loads more.

There is too much to say about SEO here, but make sure you don't go too far down the SEO rabbit hole. It's much more important to concentrate on creating great content, and building relationships with people to help you promote it, than it is to worry about SEO.

Do the basics: make sure your blog post titles and content are unique, relevant and keyword-rich (although don't 'keyword stuff'; Google doesn't like it when you go overboard). Make sure your blog and site are in a comprehensive order with logical categorization of your blog posts and a logical array of static pages. Add subheadings to your blog posts and pages, write alt (alternative) text for your images and, most important of all, create quality, relevant and shareable content.

Contact Page

Make sure you have a contact page. Go to Pages > Add New in the WordPress back-end; I use the Contact Form 7 plug-in for creating the contact form: *https://wordpress.org/plugins/contact-form-7*.

This is super easy to set up and it sends an email to you every time someone completes the form.

Spam

Spam has, unfortunately, been an ever-present pest for bloggers since the dawn of blogging. If you allow comments on your blog posts – which is great for interaction on your website – you will get spam.

There are a couple of plug-ins you can use to identify and stop the comment spam from getting through. Your new installation of WordPress will come with the plug-in Akismet installed, and you need to activate it by entering an Akismet.com API key.

I also use another free plug-in called Growmap Anti Spambot Plugin (GASP), which forces users to tick a checkbox before sending a comment – something humans can do but spambots can't: *https://wordpress.org/plugins/growmap-anti-spambot-plugin.*

Cache & Speed

You should always be looking for ways to increase your site's loading speed. Speed is of great importance to your visitors; no one wants to wait ages for a page to load. A fast-loading site will also help your rankings in the search engines.

Make sure the file sizes of the images on your website are as small as possible. There are a number of online image editors that will do this for you.

Plus there are many server-side settings that can be tweaked by your host to ensure faster page delivery. You can use Google's PageSpeed tool on your browser to see what could and should be improved on your site's pages: *https://developers.google.com/speed/pagespeed.*

You can also install a caching plug-in that will speed things up, like W3Total Cache *https://wordpress.org/plugins/w3-total-cache,* or Super Cache *https://wordpress.org/plugins/wp-super-cache.* Again, liaise with your host to find out which caching plug-in would be best for the server you're on, and which settings to use.

Lastly, you can employ the services of a Content Delivery

Network (CDN). A content delivery network is a system of web servers, located all over the world, which will supply your site from the server that's nearest to the visitor. You need to add the details of the CDN to the caching plug-in.

Security

WordPress, as I've already said, is the most widely-used software powering websites on the planet. With its increasing popularity comes increasing risk from hackers. There are several things you can do to protect yourself from attack.

The most important thing you can do is to choose hard-to-guess usernames and passwords for entry into the WordPress back-end, and to change them regularly. You must also always update all WordPress themes, plug-ins and the WordPress core as soon as they become available. WordPress tends to have four major updates a year, and sometimes other minor ones. Plug-ins and themes have regular updates too. If anything needs to be updated, you will see this in the back-end.

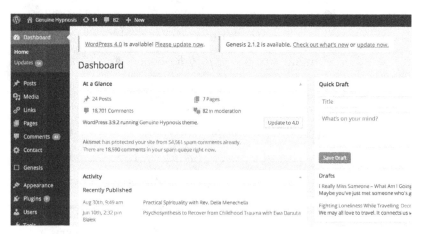

Updating is a fairly straightforward procedure. You just have to click 'Update' and follow the prompts. I don't want to put you off updating, but sometimes it breaks your site.

And to protect you from this unpleasant – although unlikely – occurrence, you must back up... (see next section).

In addition to this, there are other various tasks you can to do to protect your WordPress install. Here is a web page from WordPress about the many steps you can take to strengthen security: http://codex.wordpress.org/Hardening_WordPress

Plus, I also use the iThemes Security plug-in: *https://wordpress. org/plugins/better-wp-security*

Backing up

If anything bad happens to your site, you can revert to an earlier version, so you must create regular back-ups of your site. Your host is likely to be doing this for you, but it is such an important practice that you must do it yourself as well.

There are two elements that need to be regularly backed up: the files that sit on the server and your database.

Your files can be copied from the server via the control panel provided by your host, or by using an FTP client like FileZilla.

You can also use plug-ins to back up your database at regular intervals. These plug-ins can store database copies on your host; this doesn't provide great security as something can happen to your host's server, so it's best to get the plug-in to email you with the database back-up or to back up to a third-party cloud storage service like Dropbox. *https://wordpress.org/plugins/updraftplus*

Social media

You should make it easy for your visitors to be able to share or 'like' your blog posts. I always include the most popular social media share buttons (Twitter, Facebook, LinkedIn and, because it's Google, Google Plus). There are a variety (you could say a baffling array) of plug-ins that create these buttons.

Digg Digg, ShareThis and AddThis are examples of social media sharing plug-ins that you'll find in the WordPress plug-in repository: *https://wordpress.org/plugins.*

In addition, you should also provide links to your social media profile pages on every page of your site (in the sidebar or in the header). This way, visitors can readily subscribe to your updates on Twitter, Facebook, LinkedIn or whatever social media channel they prefer.

There is more to come about social media in the next chapter.

Not essential but nice to have

Finally, here is more functionality you can add to your WordPress install:

- Subscribe to comments – you can use a plug-in to add the ability for a visitor to subscribe to the comments on your blog posts. This means they get notified every time a new comment is added, making discussion more likely and thus increasing engagement with your site and brand.
- Favicon – a favicon is the icon image that sits up on the browser address bar or tab, and is usually a square version of the site's logo.

I'm sorry – this chapter was a dry list of things to do. But there's no avoiding the above actions. You have to implement or engage with most of those steps. Of course, you could pay someone to do this all for you, but I would challenge you to do it yourself. All the information is at your fingertips, and you will learn more by doing it yourself.

Connecting to social media

The last few years have seen the almost inexorable rise of social media. So much so, it is now almost impossible to imagine the web without the social and sharing layer of content curation.

A social media presence is essential to any brand, as it provides other channels where they can get their message out and engage with customers.

I like to schedule and automate social media posts as much as I can. Social media gurus, however, will tell you to spend time on the various channels in order to interact and engage with as much of your target market as possible. This is great if you have the time and the inclination to do this. However, I find that this time can be more effectively spent on creating content, selling products and making money. I don't have the desire to spend hours on social media.

There are also tools that schedule posts and post to multiple channels. For example, Friends+Me can put your Google Plus posts out to Facebook. *https://friendsplus.me/app*

Buffer and Hootsuite are both tools that have free versions that can schedule posts to Facebook, LinkedIn and Twitter.

Design

Whether you are setting up or improving your social media profile pages, try to brand them and keep them as consistent as possible.

Your Twitter profile page, your Google Plus profile, your YouTube channel page, your Facebook personal profile as well as your Facebook business page will all require a larger header image. Try to choose a striking image that communicates the nature of your brand on all these channels, and make sure it has your logo on it.

This consistency of branding across multiple channels is essential if your business is to be considered authentic and professional. This is why we have to ask our graphic designer to supply our logo in Adobe Illustrator and/or Adobe Photoshop versions **on a transparent background.**

Facebook

You'll need a Facebook Page as well as a personal account *https:// www.facebook.com/pages/create*; a Facebook page can collect 'likes'. Anyone who likes your page (and they can do that on your site if you wish), may see your updates in their newsfeed.

Twitter

Twitter, like all the other social networks, requires patience and engagement with other users on the channel. If you have time for this, then go for it. However, I prefer to schedule a pre-arranged set of links (with Hootsuite or Buffer) – four or five tweets for every one of my articles.

LinkedIn

LinkedIn, as everyone knows, is the more business-based social network. For this reason, LinkedIn Groups are particularly powerful. I would create a profile there if you haven't already and, this really is for the LinkedIn pros, create a company LinkedIn page for your business: *http://www.linkedin.com/company.*

Google Plus and Google Places for Business

In my opinion, Google Plus is a failed social media experiment. I jumped on it when they first started, thinking everything Google does turn into gold. It looks like I was wrong; it. Having said that, if you don't have a personal Google Plus profile, I would suggest you get one. *https://plus.google.com.*

Google Plus has pages which are similar to Facebook pages – they're for businesses rather than people. It is especially important, however, that you get a Google Plus page if you want to be found on Google Maps: *http://www.google.com/business.*

YouTube

I recommend video as a great way to tell a story and build a brand. These days, it's cheap and easy to create quality high definition videos.

What's the point of social media?

I have purposely made this section of the booklet short, as I think that a lot of time can be wasted on social media.

Yes, if you want to establish a brand you need to 'be everywhere' on social media. But brands aren't made on Facebook; they're made in the real world, by conversing with real people and real customers. And the best place to build a brand is on an estate, either real or virtual, that you own – i.e. your website and your email list.

Brand owners need to create value first and foremost in the places where they have 100% control of the brand message. Facebook, Google Plus, Twitter, YouTube and the like are platforms that can amplify that message but, ultimately, are controlled by others.

Remember to communicate your business's message primarily through your brand's main channel – its website.

But how do we get people (customers) to the website? Social media? Think again! The answer is in the next chapter.

Relationships

This is one of the most important chapters in the whole book. The subject of this chapter is critical to your website's success. It's something that is all around you, it's something you interact with every day and yet you'd sometimes think it has nothing to do with your business.

It's people. Real people. Business relationships will make or break your website and brand.

A successful, mutually beneficial business relationship with a like-minded entrepreneur will provide you with a brand ambassador, a confidant, links to your website, a potential joint venture partner and much, much more.

Do everything you can to nurture these business relationships with people who are on the same path as you – maybe a little bit ahead, maybe a little bit behind – and even if they're on a path that seems tangential to your trajectory. Connect with people with similar ideas, hopes, dreams and business goals, and keep these relationships close to your heart. You'll never know how they'll benefit you – or the other person.

Who are these people? Where do you find them?

They are everywhere.

We are all on a journey. We are going from where we are to where we think we want to go. That journey never runs on a straight line but, along the way, we meet people who are traveling with us.

Don't only try to meet people who are so fabulously successful, that you think you'll benefit from them. As I said, these relationships should be win-win. Always be thinking of how you can help these people.

Commenting

If you run into a website on your digital travels that regularly supplies you with quality information, then make sure you communicate your gratitude to the website owner in the comments after each article.

Don't just say, "Great article," but raise specific points made in the post and expand or question them. In other words, leave intelligent, engaging comments after the blog posts that you admire. As a blogger myself, I love getting comments. It means my blog posts are being read. After a few comments, the blog owner will recognize the name and visit your website. And they will know what you look like.

How? Because of the gravatar.

Gravatar

A gravatar is a globally-recognized avatar or profile photo that follows you around the Internet. Upload a beautiful image of yourself smiling into camera, and connect it to your email address at this site: *http://gravatar.com*. This will appear on every blog post that you comment on, and people will begin to know what you look like. This is an essential step in your business's branding process.

Social media

I've talked enough about how much time on social media can be wasted but, of course, another place to connect and forge win-win business relationships can be on Twitter, Facebook and the like. Indeed, on these places you can find out about people's hobbies and what they like to do away from the computer, and this can give you an extra reason to connect.

Again, first see how you can help people. Write engaging, useful messages and leave. Don't spend hours on social media.

Forums

Forums have been with us for years before the huge social channels were even thought of, and they are great places to engage and help people.

You can add a profile pic of yourself (preferably the same as your gravatar), and add a link to your website in your forum signature.

Email

The best way to connect with people online is email. Email is personal. Even with all the spam flying around these days, people still take notice of what's in their inbox.

Email the people you admire online when you think it's appropriate. Write an email with an intriguing title and an engaging conversation about a subject you're both interested in. Move forward with this person through your business journeys, while discussing the ins and outs of what you're both trying to do. This close connection will pay dividends in the long run for both parties.

Blog commenting, social media, forums and email are all great ways you can engage with like-minded business people. You are probably doing this already. Keep doing it. People will remember you and begin to consider you as an expert in your field.

However, these are all online channels. And the best channels for meeting people are offline. A face-to-face connection is always better than one made online. Here are the best ways to forge these long term business partnerships in the 'real world'.

Meetups

I remember the first business meetup I went to. I was stupidly nervous. Some of the people had been in business for longer than me and really knew what they were talking about. I was worried that they were going to think of me as an impostor.

Nobody thought of me as an impostor, of course; they were probably worrying about the same thing. And a few days later, somebody I met there sent me a client who I ended up creating a $2,000 website for.

I was hooked.

I find the website Meetup (*http://meetup.com*) great for business networking opportunities. You can go to general business meetups or gatherings that are more suited to your particular interests. Either way, you can certainly forge some great relationships here.

Conferences

Conferences are meetups on steroids. They're more expensive to go to. They may charge for attendance, you may have to travel long distances and stay in hotels. But every penny you invest will come back in terms of networking opportunities.

I have seen some bloggers catapult their businesses by attending just one conference. John Lee Dumas from Entrepreneur On Fire attended a conference to kick-start his fledging podcast and get the first few guests. It would have taken him years to get started otherwise, and now he's earning over $200,000 a month from the podcast and associated video courses.

Examples abound of how you can quickly pick up information and get contacts within an industry, in just a few days of conference networking. But remember, it's not about what people can do for you, it's about what you can do for other people.

Meet as many people as you can with the idea of helping them, and you will develop a network of like-minded entrepreneurs who will grow alongside you.

Making money

The previous chapter was supposed to be the end of this booklet!

I wanted to write a complete account of how to set up a WordPress site in the way that has been beneficial to my business.

However, in business, you must always listen to customers. So I shared the chapter headings and subtitles with a group of people I knew and asked what they thought. I kept on getting one message more than any others: "Rob, that's great, but tell us how to make money with the site!"

I have learned to listen to feedback, especially when I get the same feedback from different people again and again.

As entrepreneurs, we are always talking about the bottom line. How we can maximize revenue and reduce costs. If you go to a conference and listen to the speakers, you will hear this again and again: numbers, numbers, numbers, money, money, money.

But don't think it's all about money, because it isn't. Profit is a great metric to measure success, but it's not why we do what we do. We do what we do to help people. If we're not making any money, we're not helping anyone, so here's how you can make money with a business website.

Community

One of the objects of a business website is to create a community. A community is a collection of visitors, evangelists and customers who follow the site and its contents.

This is your tribe. They provide a great source of market research. They will tell you what they are interested in and give you ideas for content and products. One of the best methods of staying in touch with this community is via an email subscription list and, fortunately enough, this is easy to set up in your WordPress website.

Creating an email subscription list

You'll need the help of a proper email marketing company to collect email addresses and send out emails in bulk. There are many of these companies around, and most will charge for this service. Believe me, this is a small investment and you will see a return on it.

Firstly, I would recommend MailChimp *http://mailchimp.com*, which is free until you get your first 2,000 subscribers. Secondly, I use AWeber *http://aweber.com* and I pay at least $50/month for nearly 10,000 subscribers. There are several other email marketing companies out there. It doesn't matter which one you choose, as you can move your list from company to company – this email list is yours and that's why it's so valuable.

Once you have set up an account with AWeber or MailChimp, you can easily set up an email sign-up form in the sidebar, with the help of a plug-in and a widget. This can be done in a matter of minutes and there's nothing quite like the feeling of people signing up to your email list.

These are the people who have resonated with what you're saying the most. Just like with any other relationship, you should nurture your relationships with your email subscribers. Start by sending them emails! Never leave your email subscribers without an email for over two weeks. Send out links to great content on your website. Ask them about their problems and their struggles. Your email subscribers are a great source for content and product ideas.

Your email list can guarantee you sales. These people have signed up to receive emails from you, and they expect to get sold to. This is huge. Your email list is *the best source of online sales*. If you send your email subscribers a special offer, they will be more responsive than any other group of online customers.

If you are not collecting email addresses on your website, you need to start now. If you only take one piece of advice from this booklet, it would be this: collect email addresses and start a conversation with a growing audience of followers, evangelists and customers. This is the best way to grow a business online.

Consultancy (hours for dollars)

The email list is a way of making money further down the line. However, you can start making money straight away from a website, by offering **services**.

Back in 2006, I was just like any other freelancer in London. I was spending two hours a day traveling on underground trains to work at an incredibly boring job. After I'd been blogging for only a few months, I started to get inquiries from my website to do graphic design projects. This meant I could work for a few hours at home and get paid more per hour than I was getting in the office, often to do more interesting and creative work.

Providing services through a business website may not have the 'kudos' that's associated with the income of owning assets that make money for you on autopilot (more on passive income later). However, setting up a company that directly caters for clients can be a hugely lucrative venture.

It takes a bit of time and a lot of effort to find the first few clients, and it takes even more time to find the first few good clients. I found my clients through blogging and going to business meetups. Before you can kiss your boss, the commute and the cubicle goodbye, you may need to work part-time in the evenings and on weekends to build up the business to a sufficient level.

It took me two years.

I don't think that's a long time when you consider the freedom you are afforded when you are running an online serviced-based enterprise. You can work where you want, when you want and, with intelligent use of outsourcing, you can work on what you want.

Whether you are providing design, illustration, photography, development, legal or any other business services, there is one main drawback to this online business model: you are always constrained by the number of hours in a day. And, no matter how hard you work and how much you outsource, unfortunately I've found that the paltry 24 hours that we get in a day is never enough to scale the business beyond a certain point.

Fortunately, though, most other online business models *are* scalable.

Affiliate commissions

You can earn affiliate commissions for your website when a visitor purchases a product you recommend through a special link.

I can make anywhere from $20–$100 on a single click from my website to any hosting solution, premium WordPress plug-in or theme that I recommend. As long as that click results in a sale, I will receive the money automatically.

If you have decent traffic and you are a trusted brand, then you can make considerable income from affiliate commissions. In fact, many friends of mine concentrate solely on affiliate commissions for their business income.

Being an affiliate for other products has many advantages: you don't have to create a product, write a sales page, provide customer service, etc. All the 'hard work' is already done; you just have to supply traffic through an affiliate link and "watch the money roll in".

It's not as simple as that, of course. Making passive income is never easy. However, I make over $5,000 a year purely from the sales that have resulted through the affiliate links I post – mostly from blog articles I've published in previous years. You have to send a fairly large amount of quality, targeted traffic to the affiliate offer, in order to make a decent return.

If you're interested in how these affiliate links work, then go to the resources page I have created for this booklet: *http:// robcubbon.com/kindle5*. Here I recommend some hosting packages and Genesis, the premium WordPress theme. The links to these hosting packages and Genesis are affiliate links, so if you purchase a product or service through that page, I would get a proportion of that sale. You won't pay anything more. The purchasing process for the customer is exactly the same.

Advertising

Another way you can bring in passive revenue from a website is through advertising. You can sign up for Google AdSense *http://www.google.com/adsense* and place a few lines of code in a text widget on your sidebar, for example, which will display targeted ads on your website. You'll get paid each time a visitor clicks on one of these ads.

However, I have found this isn't a good business model at all. You need huge traffic to make anything like a decent return on the ads. Also, if you are trying to create a trusted business website looking for clients to buy products or services, then it looks wrong to have ads plastered all over it.

PDF e-books

My most successful passive income stream from my branded website has been info-products: e-books and video courses.

The most useful advice I can give about making info-products is this: make them! Create as many products as you can. Don't spend ages perfecting the first one. Your first one will never be your best. You will make better products over time and you'll become quicker at creating them. So start now!

My first e-book was a PDF of a few blog posts that had already been published, and it took me ages to create. I did get a few sales after I published it through my website. They weren't great sales but it was a start.

I completed my second e-book much more quickly and it sold even better.

So don't worry about your first product. Even if nobody buys it, don't worry. Failure is the best teacher. Of course, create a product that you're proud of and that will help people, but don't let that delay its completion.

Use a site like Gumroad to sell a PDF from your site: h*ttp:// gumroad.com*; you can set this up in a matter of seconds.

The first people to notify of your new book are who? You guessed it – your email list. First tell them you're writing a new book to peak their interest and ask for feedback.

You could even put a special low price when you launch it. This will go down very well with your list.

Amazon

I could write a whole book about Kindle publishing and the launch sequence, but I'll stick to a couple of paragraphs.

PDF e-books are just one format you can experiment with. You can write books for sale in the biggest bookshop in the world: Amazon.

It is ridiculously easy to write a 12,000 word e-book and sell it as a Kindle and a paperback on Amazon. This is a huge opportunity for every business that has a story to tell.

You can research the book's subject or title by asking the people on your email list or your social networks. This helps to engage people in the project before you start. Unsurprisingly, your email list plays a huge part in the procedure. Your email list will drive sales initially and this will create momentum within Amazon, which will ensure organic sales for months and years to come.

Write a few hundred words every day and, by the end of a month, you'll have your new book ready. Pass the text around to people you know, as well as a professional editor, before you publish. Feedback is gold in these situations.

Your Kindle book will sell for $2.99 and your paperback will sell for $5.99 in one of the world's biggest marketplaces, exposing you to a huge new market. These new customers will be exposed to your brand and, of course, be encouraged to sign up to your email list.

Video courses

Hopefully, by now, you're spotting a theme developing here. The email list of subscribers will feature heavily in your product creation process. The email subscribers, blog visitors and social media followers will let you know what products they would like. If they don't, ask them.

After creating a product for your site or for another platform, the email list will guarantee you an initial surge of sales. This is especially important on other platforms. If you get immediate sales after putting products on Amazon and Udemy, this looks good. The platform's algorithm sees your content as popular, and then is more likely to promote your products.

This is true if you are selling books on Amazon, and true if you're selling video courses on Udemy or on other online learning platforms.

If you are creating videos on YouTube (and I would advise you to do so), then I recommend that you create some courses for Udemy as well. Udemy is the market leader in career skills asynchronous learning. It has been very useful for my web and graphic design brand. It's a great platform for a brand to create premium video training, because it shows authority. Also, people pay more for video courses than they do for e-books.

You can sell video courses from your site using WordPress membership plug-ins such as WishList Member or MemberMouse. There is also a plethora of online learning platforms where you can sell branded videos. Udemy, as I've already mentioned, is the market leader, but I have also sold courses on Skillfeed and Skillshare.

Creating videos is surprisingly easy. You can do most of the shooting and editing using screencasting software such as ScreenFlow (Mac) or Camtasia (PC). Decent microphones can be picked up for $50-100.

None of the online learning platforms insist on any exclusivity. So you can have courses on Udemy and your own website. You can make a decent amount of money on all these platforms. Plus a site like Udemy, with four million paying users, exposes your brand to a targeted audience of buyers.

Both e-books and video courses can be used as lead generation tools. They can add buyers to a funnel that you can sell to further down the line. There is no better lead than a customer who has already bought from you.

Software as a Service (SaaS)

An even better model for earning passive income from a website is Software as a Service. Examples of SaaS applications would be cloud-based solutions for email marketing, accounting, collaboration and customer relations.

The advantages of creating a SaaS app would be the ongoing revenue, as they typically charge a monthly fee for access to the software. This income model would be the most expensive to set up, but it is potentially the most profitable.

There are other ways to generate income from a website, but I hope this gives you a few ideas for how you can grow your brand and website in the future.

Putting it all together

I hope the readers of this little book will be inspired to create brands and businesses with WordPress sites, just as I have.

You don't have to be too technical to do this, you don't have to have a mind-blowingly original business idea and you don't have to be rich. Anyone can create a successful business online. *You* can do it.

If there's one word that is more important than all others in online business, it's this one: consistency.

You should be consistently working on your website, consistently creating quality content on it, consistently collecting email addresses, consistently emailing them and consistently providing quality services and/or products.

The worst thing you can do is write one blog article every month for a year, and then give up. Or lock yourself away in an attic for months and months, working on your first big product, with no feedback from an audience. Consistent content creation provides constant feedback and encouragement. You are unlikely to become discouraged if you take a small step every single day and have people encouraging you to go further.

Once you have a site up and running, try to complete a single task every day to improve it. You could: answer a comment, improve the functionality by adding a plug-in, write a blog post, make an improvement to the site loading speed, etc.

If you see improvements in your Google Analytics, feedback from your customers or engagement with your audience, however small at first, it means you are on the correct path and you have to keep going.

Do something to create wealth every day: either write 500 words of an e-book or record and edit five minutes of a video course – after a month you'll have written a book or created a video course. Both of these are income-earning assets that also increase your following and brand awareness.

In this way, you will be secured in an ever-spiraling virtuous circle: you create content that builds a following; the following lets you know of great new product ideas; you create these products; these products increase your following, that lets you know of even better product ideas... and so it goes on.

You'll be helping people in the way you have been helped by the great information we have at our fingertips online. It's good for you and good for the world.

Finally, after reading all the advice I've given you, there's only one thing left to do: **take action!**

Thank you!

Thank you so much for reading my booklet.

What could be better than doing something you love every day?

I love helping people with their businesses. Nothing would make me happier than if this booklet could help you.

Maybe you felt inspired to start your own brand and business website. Maybe you already have a business or a website and this has helped you in some way.

If so, then please consider leaving a review at Amazon. Positive reviews really help get the message out there and I'd be extremely grateful if you would pen an honest review and tell me what you thought about the book.

If you have any questions please pop along to *my website* at *http://robcubbon.com* and leave a comment on one of the articles or drop me a line. And, remember, you can *sign up to my email list* to receive free newsletter, Kindles and e-books. Sign up here: *http://robcubbon.com/free*

Cheers,

Rob Cubbon

PS. Keep reading, there's loads more ways I can help you!

Videos and books

Video courses

I have been making various video courses for the last two years. They are on the subjects of web design, running an online business and online marketing generally. You can join my membership site at *http://learn.robcubbon.com* and view all these courses. Here are some of my courses:

Business: *Make Money Running A Web Design Business*
How to make money by running a successful web design business from home and charging 4-figures plus for every website. How to set up a business, how to find clients and how to run the business successfully.

WordPress (advanced): *Creating a Web Design Business Website*
Learn how to design and develop this site – *Crea8iveDesigns. com* – the website of a fictitious design company.

Marketing & Promotion: *Build My Brand: Blogging, SEO, Social Media & Relationships*
This course shows you how to get noticed online with blogging, social media, SEO and by building win-win relationships with other business people in your niche. It proves the success of this model by ranking for buying keywords on a new site.

Free course: *Talking To Clients: An Introduction To Website Building*

Learn how to talk to a new client. This course shows me talking to Nura Nash about her new website.

Web design: *Designing A Website in Photoshop, Illustrator (& GIMP)*

This course shows you how to "mock-up" or create a visual of a website before developing it in Photoshop, Illustrator (& GIMP). This is mostly based around the creation of Nura Nash's website.

WordPress (intermediate): *Create A Custom Responsive WordPress Website For A Client*

Learn how to create this website *NuraHNash.com* with WordPress and the Genesis theme framework.

Design: *Photoshop: Hands-on Graphic and Web Design*

The most important Photoshop techniques you'll need while doing graphic design jobs for print and web.

Free course: Email Marketing: *How To Build an Email List of Customers*

Step-by-step instructions on how to collect emails, create a relationship with your subscribers and grow your business.

You can join my membership site and view all these courses at *http://learn.robcubbon.com*

Other books I've written

I have also written some other booklet's that have been very well reviewed, I'm pleased to say.

Running A Web Design Business From Home

The book explains how to set up your business from home – the hardware and software you'll need. I also write about how you get long term, quality clients that will recommend you and give you on-going work. We also talk about how to run web design projects as well as the diversification of your business going forward.

It's not a "get rich quick" book. You are encouraged to start in your spare time and slowly but surely build up your long-term professional contacts and online authority. This will provide you with a solid base for whatever you want to achieve with your online business in the future.

Here's what one reviewer said: I love how simply Rob explains everything. I've taken a few of his e-courses, and jumped on this book when it came out. It's a quick-read, but extremely useful. Rob does a great job of skipping the fluff and getting to the point--while keeping it interesting and upbeat. Even though I've been running my own web design company for two years now, Rob's tips are great and he gave me some great ideas to put into practice!

You can get *Running A Web Design Business From Home* here. *http://www.amzn.com/B00G5IV01Y*

How To Sell Video Courses Online

I make over $5000 passive income every month from video tutorials and you can too.

This book explains: how to research the content and title of your courses, technical information about video course creation, advice on how to create your first course, how to market your course, and loads more.

The world is changing. Education is changing. There is a HUGE demand for career skills courses online. Once you have created a course it can earn you substantial money every month for years to come.

Plus you will enjoy the process of making the course and the feedback from the students. Course creation is not only very satisfying it also helps builds your brand as an authority within your niche. Here's a review: *In all his books and blog articles, Rob Cubbon's writing reflects his down-to-earth honesty, superb clarity and considerable experience. In this work, Rob shows us how to record video courses once, make them available on the internet and earn a passive income from them for months or years afterwards. As an online instructor for nearly five years myself, I was not only informed, I was also inspired.*

Isn't that wonderful! I deeply appreciate all the reviews I get. If you've enjoyed this book, it would be great if you could give me a review. I would be so, so grateful.

You can get *How To Sell Video Courses Online* here. *http://www.amzn.com/B00H2OEDDM*

Build a Brand, Create Products and Earn Passive Income

This is a blueprint for **online success**. It's everything I've learned during a decade of living online.

This is not a get-rich-quick book. However, if you do what it says, you will make money online.

You will also grow an authoritative personal brand, that will benefit both you and your businesses for years to come.

I'm going to tell you how to enjoy creating regular content that will be consumed by a growing community of adoring fans and how to unlock the secrets of social media and email marketing to ask them what they want. And then, how to create products (books, podcasts, videos) to sell to them and others.

So, to re-cap: Your brand is followed by an audience. They tell you what they want, you build it and they buy it. And you keep going. It's very simple.

And there's more good news: you won't have to spend any money.

At the end, I'm going to send you on your way with my strategy ingrained in your mind. This will help you to build your brand, create products and earn passive income. Plus you'll be able to keep going. My strategy ensures there's always more in the tank to give. Creativity breeds creativity.

You will enjoy creating content. So, let's get going!

Buy **Build a Brand, Create Products and Earn Passive Income** in the US here: *http://www.amazon.com/dp/ B00LTWLSE0*

Buy **Build a Brand, Create Products and Earn Passive Income** in the UK here: *http://www.amazon.co.uk/dp/ B00LTWLSE0*

Excerpt from: From Freelancer to Entrepreneur: Escaping work and finding happiness

This is a semi-autobiographical book about how I was lost professional, emotionally and spiritually and how, bit by bit, I was able to set up my own business and work from home – with a few ups and downs along the way.

You can buy this book on Amazon US: From Freelancer to Entrepreneur: Escaping work and finding happiness
http://www.amazon.com/dp/B00J7BK4MC/

You can buy this book on Amazon UK: From Freelancer to Entrepreneur: Escaping work and finding happiness
http://www.amazon.co.uk/dp/B00J7BK4MC/

Chapter 1: "More by accident than by design"

I'm a very lucky man.

I was born in England to fairly well-off parents. I have both my arms and legs. I possess modest intelligence, near perfect eyesight, and I can vaguely string an English sentence together in both spoken and written form.

However, I didn't always think I was lucky. In fact, my head used to be filled with thoughts of how unlucky I was: *If only I were better looking; If only I'd been more popular at school; If only I'd been born with more innate talent.*

This book is the story of how, in only a few years, I went from being a barely employable Mac monkey—trudging joylessly around London offices, performing mind-numbingly repetitive tasks that no one else wanted to do—to running a successful graphic design business. It doesn't centre, as a lot of books do, around one transformative life-changing moment. Instead, this book contains a whole host of them.

There have been many coincidences, pieces of advice, and much wonderful happenstance. My assertion that "I am a lucky man" has actually become more true during the writing of this book.

And there are more general instances of luck.

My consciousness has attached itself to a human at this moment. That's lucky; I would hate to have been a slug, although I've always thought being an albatross would be kind of cool.

I am alive in 2014. I am alive in the Internet age, and I have the opportunity to set up an online business and to craft my own lifestyle. A few years ago, this wouldn't have been possible. I would have had to do what I was told by the boss/factory owner/ feudal landlord/lord/chief/king.

And then there are more general instances of good luck. For example, my freelance work meant I had time to work at home building up my business whilst I had money coming in; it didn't matter that the business didn't bring in much in the first two years. In 2005, I was introduced to WordPress, the most popular website content management system (CMS). I started blogging in 2006. My website looked shockingly bad from 2005–2007, but it didn't matter because the recession hadn't happened yet.

I have learned to be grateful. I occasionally wake up and thank the universe for my position within and experience of it.

Chapter 2: Starting work

If you're older than eighteen, what would be the one thing you'd say to your eighteen-year-old self?

Yeah, I know; "buy Apple stock" would be obvious. But I would actually say, "don't bother going to college; leave that crappy band you play guitar for; don't bother getting a job. Just do what you want!"

Our schools, families, and backgrounds pre-program us, and we spend our whole lives trying to unlearn it.

That was certainly the case for me when, aged twenty-one and virtually unemployable, I limped towards the end of my further education with a humanities degree from a lesser-known London University.

I eventually found a job, and this was—and always will be—my only ever job, as a picture researcher for a magazine aimed at the over-fifties. This was hardly the glamorous media career I'd had in mind. It was the only thing I could get in the early nineties, when the UK was going through another recession, and I was pleased with it.

The day-to-day work at that magazine would seem industrial today, and it's hard to imagine that it was only twenty years ago. But the worst thing about my old job wasn't the mind-numbing, pointless, repetitive to-ing and fro-ing. No, it was the boss.

She seemed nice enough at first, but I'd noticed a certain trepidation in the other staff towards her. It wasn't long before I found out why. This superficially pleasant and charming fifty-something lady could morph into a mad dictator of Hitleresque proportions at the drop of a hat. She spent most of the day criticising, haranguing, and patronising her staff. This was a period of particularly bad recession for the middle class. Those who had jobs would hold onto them for fear of losing the homes and stability they'd spent their whole lives working towards.

The women in that office used to tell me that I was lucky to be a man because I missed the worst of her attacks.

But I'd seen enough. After a few months I was ready to get out of there. I desperately looked around for another job, but I couldn't find one. The recession had hit hard and I didn't have the skills, experience, or training that employers were looking for. Who does at twenty-one?

For two more years I was stuck in this nightmare job. It would have been difficult for me to believe this at the time, but that was probably the most educational period of my professional life. Why? The experience was so bad that it led me towards becoming an entrepreneur.

The education came from looking at the fear on my poor colleagues' faces. Frightened of doing anything wrong and suffering public humiliation at the hands of the boss. I knew I could never end up like them. At one stage, I thought I'd rather be homeless and unemployed, but thankfully, I never had to find out.

Chapter 3: Stagnation

Let's fast-forward ten years.

It's a funny thing time, isn't it?

We work hours and hours of it; we suffer it, resent it, and curse it for moving so damn slow. Then we yearn to spend quality time with our loved ones—and then quality time goes by too quickly. We spend time looking forward to holiday time, enjoy thinking about the good times, complain about the bad times. We tell ourselves, if only this and that didn't bother us, we'd have more good times.

At least, that was my relationship with time back in 2004. Ten years ago I was living on my own in a flat in north London. Travelling on the underground train to my place of work along with a million other people, head down in the morning paper, not questioning my existence. I didn't think twice about the need to make money by working at some faceless corporation, without meaning, without purpose.

Everybody has to work; you've got to pay the bills. How else are you going to live your life?

Despite thinking that this was the only answer, I didn't suffer in silence. No, my head and conversation was full of negative observations about work.

I hated work. I hated the pettiness. I hated the falseness. I hated the fact that other people (increasingly *younger* people) could tell me what to do. Even worse, they could *criticise* my work!

You can buy this book on Amazon US: From Freelancer to Entrepreneur: Escaping work and finding happiness *http://www.amazon.com/dp/B00J7BK4MC/*

You can buy this book on Amazon UK: From Freelancer to Entrepreneur: Escaping work and finding happiness *http://www.amazon.co.uk/dp/B00J7BK4MC/*

Create the Website You Want with WordPress:

A how-to guide for building a branded business asset

By Rob Cubbon

Published By: Rob Cubbon Ltd *RobCubbon.com*

publication to ensure its accuracy.

The reader assumes all responsibility for the use of the information within this report.

If you do not accept the terms of this agreement, please return the product immediately for a full refund, at which point you must destroy any copies of the publication in your possession.

Peace!

www.ingramcontent.com/pod-product-compliance
Lightning Source LLC
Chambersburg PA
CBHW060949050326
40689CB00012B/2614